Be Happy Always

This Notebook Belongs To:

....

....

....

....

....

....

....

....

....

If Lost
Please Return To :

Name : ....

Email : ....

Phon : ....

....

Made in the USA
Monee, IL
08 April 2021

65168501R00069